Rental Property Maintenance Checklist

Carter Hayes

Contents

Chapter One

Maintenance is Profit

Most landlords don't lose money because of bad tenants. They lose money because they ignore small problems until they turn into expensive ones.

A ten-dollar supply line becomes a five-thousand-dollar insurance claim.

A clogged dryer vent becomes a fire hazard.

A loose shingle becomes interior water damage.

Maintenance is not an expense.

It is protection.

If you treat your rental like a paycheck instead of a property, you will always be reacting.

If you treat it like an asset, you will stay ahead of problems.

This book is about staying ahead.

The Truth About Rental Maintenance

Here's what most new landlords get wrong:

They wait.

They wait until a tenant calls.

They wait until something breaks.

They wait until they see water on the floor.

By the time a tenant notices a problem, it has already been a problem for a while.

Preventative maintenance is simple.

You find small issues before they become expensive ones.

That's it.

No complicated systems.

No expensive software.

No contractor license required.

Just consistency.

Reactive vs Preventative

There are two types of landlords.

The Reactive Landlord

Waits for complaints

Patches instead of fixes

Delays HVAC servicing

Ignores exterior inspections

Fixes only what is visible

The result:

Higher repair costs.

Frustrated tenants.

More emergency calls.

Lower long-term property value.

The Preventative Landlord

Inspects regularly

Tracks maintenance dates

Services major systems on schedule

Fixes small problems immediately

Budgets for upkeep

The result:

Lower long-term costs.

Longer tenant stays.

Fewer midnight phone calls.

Stronger resale value.

It is not about being handy.

It is about being disciplined.

Why Deferred Maintenance Destroys ROI

Let's break this down in plain numbers.

You skip servicing the HVAC for three years.

You save maybe one hundred fifty dollars per year.

Then the blower motor fails in the middle of July.

Now you are dealing with:

Emergency service fees

After-hours charges

An angry tenant

Possibly a hotel reimbursement

Suddenly you are spending one thousand dollars or more.

The money you "saved" just cost you triple.

Deferred maintenance quietly eats profit.

You will not see it on a spreadsheet until it is too late.

Your Property Is a System

A rental property is not just walls and rent checks.

It is a system made up of:

Roof

Plumbing

Electrical

HVAC

Appliances

Exterior drainage

Structural components

If one part fails, it stresses another.

Clogged gutters lead to fascia rot.

Poor grading leads to foundation cracks.

Neglected caulking leads to interior water damage.

Maintenance protects the system.

Protect the system and you protect the income.

The Rule of Small Problems

Here is a rule that will protect your investment long term.

Fix small problems immediately.

Not next month.

Not when rent clears.

Not when you "have time."

Immediately.

Small problems are cheap.

Big problems are not.

The Maintenance Mindset

If you own rentals, you are not just a landlord.

You are:

An asset manager

A risk manager

A systems manager

Your job is not just to collect rent.

Your job is to protect the building that produces rent.

Once you understand that, maintenance stops feeling like a chore.

It becomes strategy.

What This Book Will Give You

This book is not theory.

You are going to get:

Monthly checklists

Quarterly inspections

Seasonal maintenance plans

Move-in and move-out systems

Emergency prevention steps

An annual inspection structure

You do not need to be a contractor.

You just need a system.

Once you have one, maintenance becomes predictable instead of stressful.

And predictable is profitable.

Chapter Two

The Monthly Maintenance Checklist

Monthly maintenance is not about doing major repairs. It is about catching small problems before they become expensive ones.

This should take you thirty to sixty minutes per property.

No skipping months. No excuses.

If you own multiple units, block one day each month and run the system the same way every time.

Consistency protects profit.

HVAC System

Your HVAC system is one of the most expensive components in the property.

Neglecting it is one of the fastest ways to burn money.

Monthly tasks:

Replace or inspect air filters

Check for unusual noises while running

Make sure return vents are not blocked

Confirm thermostat is working properly

Look for water around the indoor unit

Restricted airflow kills systems.

A cheap filter protects an expensive repair.

Plumbing Quick Check

Water damage destroys profit quietly.

You are checking for leaks. That is it.

Monthly tasks:

Inspect under all sinks for moisture

Check supply lines for corrosion or swelling

Look behind toilets for active leaks

Run all faucets and check drainage speed

Inspect around the water heater base

If you see moisture, address it immediately.

Water problems never get cheaper with time.

Safety Devices

These are liability items.

Do not skip them.

Monthly tasks:

Test all smoke detectors

Test carbon monoxide detectors

Inspect fire extinguishers

Confirm GFCI outlets trip and reset properly

Check exterior security lighting

A working detector costs very little.

A lawsuit costs a lot.

Exterior Walk-Around

Do not rely on tenants to report exterior issues.

Do your own inspection.

Monthly tasks:

Walk the perimeter of the property

Look for roof damage from ground level

Check siding for cracks or separation

Inspect foundation for new cracks

Make sure grading slopes away from the structure

You are looking for changes.

Changes mean movement.

Movement means future repair.

Appliances

Appliances protect tenant satisfaction.

When they fail, frustration follows fast.

Monthly tasks:

Run dishwasher briefly

Check refrigerator door seals

Test stove burners and oven heat

Inspect washing machine hoses

Make sure dryer vent is not crushed or restricted

Most appliance failures show warning signs before complete failure.

Listen for them.

Drainage and Moisture

Water around the exterior turns into structural damage if ignored.

Monthly tasks:

Check downspouts for blockage

Confirm water flows away from foundation

Look for pooling water after rain

Inspect window seals

Check basement or crawl space for dampness

Moisture is the enemy of long-term property value.

Control moisture and you control cost.

Interior Condition Check

Even good tenants create small wear and tear.

Catch it early.

Monthly tasks:

Look for wall cracks

Inspect ceilings for stains

Check doors for sticking

Look for loose trim

Confirm windows open and close properly

Small cosmetic issues often reveal bigger structural shifts.

Do not ignore patterns.

Monthly Documentation Rule

If something looks questionable:

Take a photo.

Log the date.

Schedule the repair if needed.

Documentation protects you during disputes.

Documentation protects profit.

Chapter Three

The Quarterly Maintenance Checklist

M onthly maintenance catches surface issues. Quarterly maintenance protects structure and major systems.

These inspections go deeper.

Plan for ninety minutes to two hours per property.

Do this every three months without fail.

Seasonal changes are when damage happens.

Roof and Gutter Inspection

Your roof protects everything under it.

You are not climbing it unless trained. This is a visual inspection from the ground or ladder at the edge only.

Quarterly tasks:

Look for missing or curling shingles

Check for sagging areas

Inspect flashing around vents and chimneys

Clear debris from gutters

Make sure downspouts are firmly attached

Clogged gutters cause fascia rot and foundation problems.

Water must move away from the structure.

Exterior Seals and Caulking

Small gaps turn into water intrusion.

Quarterly tasks:

Inspect window caulking

Check door weather stripping

Look for cracks in exterior sealants

Inspect siding joints

Seal visible gaps immediately

Caulk is cheap.

Interior water damage is not.

Electrical System Check

Electrical issues are often invisible until failure.

Quarterly tasks:

Test GFCI outlets

Test AFCI breakers if installed

Look for warm or discolored outlets

Confirm breaker panel labeling is clear

Check exterior outlets for weather protection

Burn marks mean heat.

Heat means danger.

Do not ignore electrical warning signs.

Dryer Vent and Exhaust Systems

Lint buildup is a fire hazard.

Quarterly tasks:

Inspect dryer vent for blockage

Confirm exterior flap opens when dryer runs

Clean accessible lint buildup

Check bathroom exhaust fans for airflow

Inspect kitchen hood vent operation

Restricted airflow leads to overheating.

Overheating leads to damage.

HVAC Performance Check

This is not a full service, but a performance review.

Quarterly tasks:

Listen for new noises

Check airflow from vents

Confirm consistent temperature distribution

Inspect outdoor condenser for debris

Make sure vegetation is trimmed away

Poor airflow stresses the system.

Stressed systems fail early.

Foundation and Structural Walk

Movement starts small.

Quarterly tasks:

Look for new cracks in foundation

Check for sticking doors or windows

Inspect garage slab for separation

Look for uneven settling

Confirm crawl space ventilation is clear

Structural shifts reveal themselves through patterns.

Pay attention to changes.

Pest Activity Check

Pests cause hidden damage.

Quarterly tasks:

Look for droppings in attic or crawl space

Inspect wood for chew marks

Check for ant or termite trails

Confirm exterior penetrations are sealed

Inspect trash storage areas

Pest damage spreads quickly.

Early detection keeps it manageable.

Quarterly Documentation Rule

After each quarterly inspection:

Log the date

Note any changes

Photograph problem areas

Schedule repairs within seven days

Delaying repair after discovery defeats the purpose of inspection.

Quarterly maintenance protects long-term asset value.

It separates disciplined landlords from reactive ones.

Chapter Four

The Biannual Maintenance Checklist

Biannual maintenance is where you protect the expensive systems.

This is not a quick walk-through.

This is deeper servicing done twice per year.

Schedule it:

Once in the spring

Once in the fall

Season changes stress buildings.

This is where you get ahead of breakdowns.

Professional HVAC Service

This is not optional.

Twice per year:

Schedule full HVAC tune-up

Inspect blower motor and capacitor

Check refrigerant levels

Clean condenser coils

Inspect heat exchanger

Test safety shutoffs

Skipping service shortens system life.

A serviced system lasts years longer.

That difference is profit.

Water Heater Service

Water heaters quietly fail.

Twice per year:

Flush sediment from tank

Inspect pressure relief valve

Check for corrosion at fittings

Inspect venting system

Confirm proper temperature setting

Sediment buildup destroys heating elements.

Flush it before it costs you a replacement.

Full Gutter Cleaning

Even if you checked them quarterly.

Twice per year:

Remove all debris

Flush downspouts

Inspect for separation

Check for rust or sagging

Confirm proper drainage slope

Overflowing gutters damage siding and foundations.

Water must move away from the structure.

Appliance Deep Inspection

Twice per year:

Pull refrigerator and vacuum coils

Inspect dishwasher hoses

Check washing machine drain lines

Inspect dryer vent internally

Confirm stove and oven heating evenly

Appliance neglect shortens lifespan.

Short lifespan increases turnover costs.

Caulking and Sealant Refresh

Sun and temperature break down sealants.

Twice per year:

Reapply caulk where cracking appears

Seal exterior penetrations

Check around exterior lighting fixtures

Inspect roof flashing seals

Inspect bathroom and kitchen silicone joints

Seals fail slowly.

Water damage happens fast.

Pest Treatment

Even if no visible activity.

Twice per year:

Apply perimeter pest treatment

Inspect attic insulation for disturbance

Check crawl space for nesting

Seal exterior cracks

Inspect foundation penetrations

Preventing pests is cheaper than repairing damage.

Attic and Ventilation Check

Heat buildup destroys roofing materials.

Twice per year:

Inspect attic ventilation

Check for moisture stains

Confirm insulation coverage

Look for signs of roof leaks

Ensure vents are not blocked

Proper airflow extends roof life.

Roof replacement is expensive.

Biannual Documentation Rule

After each service:

Save all receipts

Log service dates

Photograph serviced systems

Track next service due date

This protects you during:

Insurance claims

Tenant disputes

Property resale

Documentation adds credibility.

Biannual maintenance protects major systems.

Major systems are what destroy budgets when ignored.

Discipline here separates amateurs from professionals.

Chapter Five

The Annual Full Property Inspection

Once per year, you do a full reset.

This is not a quick walk-through.

This is a full-property evaluation.

You are reviewing:

Condition

Safety

Wear and tear

Future repairs

Budget forecasting

This inspection protects next year's profit.

Block at least two to three hours per property.

Do not rush it.

Full Interior Walk-Through

You are looking for patterns.

Not just damage. Patterns.

Annual tasks:

Inspect all walls for cracks or movement

Check ceilings for stains or sagging

Inspect flooring for soft spots

Test all doors and locks

Check window operation and seals

Inspect baseboards and trim

Look for signs of moisture or mold

Patterns reveal structural shifts.

A single crack may mean nothing.

A spreading crack means movement.

Plumbing System Review

Go deeper than monthly checks.

Annual tasks:

Inspect shut-off valves

Check for slow drains

Inspect exposed pipes for corrosion

Test water pressure

Inspect under tubs and showers if accessible

Small corrosion now becomes pipe failure later.

Replace aging supply lines before they fail.

Electrical System Review

Electrical issues rarely give second chances.

Annual tasks:

Inspect breaker panel for corrosion

Tighten accessible terminal connections if qualified

Replace damaged outlet covers

Check for outdated wiring

Inspect exterior fixtures

If you are unsure, hire a licensed electrician.

Electrical fires destroy buildings.

Roof and Structural Review

If needed, bring in a professional.

Annual tasks:

Schedule professional roof inspection

Inspect attic framing

Check for sagging roof lines

Inspect foundation walls

Check exterior stair and deck stability

Deck failures create liability.

Liability destroys profit.

Exterior and Drainage Review

Annual tasks:

Inspect grading around foundation

Check for soil erosion

Inspect driveway and walkway cracks

Inspect fence stability

Check retaining walls

Drainage protects structure.

Structure protects value.

HVAC and Mechanical Forecast

Beyond servicing, forecast replacement.

Annual tasks:

Check HVAC age and lifespan

Evaluate performance efficiency

Inspect water heater age

Inspect major appliance age

Plan for future replacement

If HVAC is twelve years old, prepare.

If water heater is nearing lifespan, budget.

Planned replacement is controlled cost.

Emergency replacement is chaos.

Capital Expense Planning

This is where disciplined landlords win.

After inspection:

Estimate repairs needed within twelve months

Estimate replacements within three to five years

Create a reserve budget

Allocate monthly savings toward future repairs

Every property should have a repair reserve.

No reserve means panic when failure happens.

Tenant Condition Evaluation

If property is occupied:

Document tenant-caused damage

Evaluate cleanliness

Review lease compliance

Address small violations early

Annual inspections reduce turnover damage.

Tenants maintain better when they know you inspect.

Annual Documentation Rule

After inspection:

Create a written summary

Save all photos

Update maintenance log

Schedule necessary repairs within thirty days

Annual inspections turn landlords into operators.

Operators build portfolios.

Reactive landlords stay stressed.

This chapter protects the long game.

Annual inspection is not optional.

It is how you control the next year before it controls you.

The Move-In Inspection System

Move-in is where protection begins.

If you skip this step, you lose leverage later.

This inspection protects you from:

False damage claims

Security deposit disputes

Maintenance confusion

Tenant neglect

You are not just handing over keys.

You are documenting condition.

The Purpose of a Move-In Inspection

The move-in inspection creates a baseline.

Without a baseline, you cannot prove damage later.

This protects:

Your property

Your time

Your money

Everything must be documented before the tenant fully occupies the unit.

Schedule the Inspection Properly

Do not rush this.

Best practice:

Inspect after cleaning is complete

Inspect before tenant moves belongings in

Walk the property with the tenant

Have both parties sign documentation

Never rely on memory.

Documentation wins disputes.

Exterior Move-In Checklist

Before stepping inside:

Photograph entire exterior

Photograph roof condition from ground

Inspect siding condition

Photograph driveway and walkway condition

Check fencing and gates

Document landscaping condition

Take wide photos and close-up photos.

More documentation is better than less.

Interior General Condition

Room-by-room inspection.

Move methodically.

For each room:

Photograph walls

Photograph ceilings

Photograph floors

Check door operation

Check windows

Inspect trim and baseboards

Open and close everything.

Test everything.

Assume nothing.

Kitchen Inspection

The kitchen causes the most disputes.

Document carefully.

Photograph inside refrigerator

Photograph inside oven

Test stove burners

Run dishwasher briefly

Inspect sink for leaks

Photograph cabinet interiors

Clean condition should be obvious in photos.

Bathroom Inspection

Water damage often starts here.

Photograph tub and shower

Inspect caulking

Check toilet stability

Run sink and shower

Check exhaust fan operation

Inspect under sink

Take close-up photos of grout and fixtures.

Appliance Documentation

Appliance disputes are common.

For each appliance:

Photograph model and serial number

Photograph condition

Confirm operation

Document existing wear

This protects you from replacement arguments later.

HVAC and Mechanical

Test heating and cooling

Photograph thermostat

Confirm filter is new

Check water heater operation

Document breaker panel condition

If possible, record short video clips.

Video adds protection.

Safety Verification

Test smoke detectors

Test carbon monoxide detectors

Verify fire extinguisher present

Confirm locks function properly

Safety failures become legal problems.

Tenant Sign-Off

After inspection:

Provide tenant copy of inspection form

Allow tenant to note concerns

Both parties sign and date

Save digital copy

Store photos securely

Never skip the signature.

A signed document protects you.

The Move-In Rule

If it is not documented, it did not exist.

Assume any undocumented damage will be blamed on you later.

Documentation protects the security deposit.

Documentation protects relationships.

Documentation protects profit.

Move-in inspections take time.

Disputes take longer.

Choose discipline now instead of stress later.

Chapter Seven

The Move-Out Damage Assessment System

M ove-out is not emotional.

It is procedural.

You are not arguing.

You are documenting.

This process determines:

Security deposit returns

Repair timelines

Turnover costs

Tenant reputation

If you rush this step, you lose leverage.

Slow down. Be thorough.

Schedule the Inspection Properly

Best practice:

Inspect immediately after keys are returned

Inspect before cleaners or contractors enter

Bring your original move-in documentation

Bring your camera

You are comparing condition against the baseline.

That baseline is your protection.

Exterior Damage Assessment

Start outside.

Look for changes from move-in.

Inspect siding for new damage

Check for broken exterior fixtures

Inspect landscaping damage

Check driveway stains

Inspect fence and gates

Photograph everything.

Wide shot first.

Close-up second.

Interior General Condition

Walk room by room.

Be systematic.

For each room:

Photograph walls

Photograph ceilings

Inspect flooring for stains or tears

Check doors and locks

Inspect window glass and screens

Look for unauthorized modifications

Normal wear and tear is expected.

Damage is different.

Know the difference.

Kitchen Condition Review

The kitchen often carries the highest turnover cost.

Check:

Appliance cleanliness

Broken handles or knobs

Grease buildup

Cabinet damage

Countertop chips or burns

Sink condition

Compare to move-in photos.

If it was clean and intact at move-in, it should be returned in similar condition minus normal wear.

Bathroom Condition Review

Bathrooms reveal neglect quickly.

Check:

Caulking damage

Mold from poor ventilation

Cracked tiles

Broken fixtures

Excessive staining

Toilet stability

Water damage caused by tenant neglect is not normal wear.

Document it clearly.

Appliance Inspection

For each appliance:

Test operation

Check for unusual noise

Inspect hoses and connections

Photograph condition

Compare serial numbers if necessary

Appliance abuse is chargeable.

Age-related failure is not.

Be fair. Be consistent.

Hidden Damage Check

Some damage only shows after tenants leave.

Look for:

Holes behind furniture

Pet damage to baseboards

Odors from carpet

Unauthorized painting

Damaged blinds

Inspect slowly.

Rushed inspections miss money.

Security Deposit Decision Process

After inspection:

Review original move-in documentation

Separate normal wear from damage

Estimate repair cost

Collect contractor bids if needed

Itemize deductions clearly

Do not guess.

Use real numbers.

Transparency prevents disputes.

Documentation and Communication

After assessment:

Create written damage report

Attach photo evidence

Provide itemized list of deductions

Send within legal timeline required by your state

Follow your state's security deposit laws strictly.

Missed deadlines can cost you the entire deposit.

The Move-Out Rule

Be professional.

Be calm.

Be consistent.

Never argue on site.

Let documentation speak.

Fair landlords build reputations.

Emotional landlords create problems.

Turnover is part of the business.

But uncontrolled turnover costs kill profit.

Disciplined move-out systems protect your margins.

Chapter Eight

The Emergency Repair Prevention Plan

E mergency calls destroy profit.

They also destroy peace of mind.

Most emergencies are not random.

They are ignored warning signs.

This chapter is about reducing midnight phone calls before they happen.

You cannot eliminate every emergency.

But you can eliminate most of them.

What Qualifies as a True Emergency

Not every repair is urgent.

A true emergency includes:

Active water leak

No heat in freezing weather

Electrical fire risk

Sewage backup

Gas leak

Total power loss

A dripping faucet is not an emergency.

A broken cabinet hinge is not an emergency.

Train your tenants to understand the difference.

The Top Causes of Rental Emergencies

Most emergency repairs come from:

Plumbing failures

HVAC breakdowns

Electrical overloads

Roof leaks

Clogged sewer lines

Appliance failures

Almost all of these give warning signs.

You prevent emergencies by responding early to minor complaints.

Plumbing Emergency Prevention

Water damage is the most expensive emergency.

Prevent it by:

Replacing old supply lines proactively

Inspecting shut-off valves annually

Educating tenants on what not to flush

Installing leak detectors near water heaters

Checking water pressure regularly

High water pressure destroys plumbing systems.

Install pressure regulators if needed.

HVAC Emergency Prevention

Heating and cooling failures create panic.

Prevent them by:

Servicing HVAC twice per year

Replacing filters consistently

Monitoring system age

Budgeting for replacement before failure

Educating tenants not to block vents

If HVAC is near end of life, plan replacement before peak season.

Emergency replacement costs more.

Electrical Emergency Prevention

Electrical failures can become dangerous fast.

Prevent them by:

Replacing outdated panels

Upgrading damaged wiring

Inspecting outlets for heat marks

Installing surge protection

Avoiding overloaded circuits

If a tenant reports flickering lights, investigate immediately.

That is a warning sign.

Roof and Water Intrusion Prevention

Roof leaks rarely start as major leaks.

Prevent them by:

Inspecting roof quarterly

Clearing gutters regularly

Checking attic for moisture

Repairing minor flashing issues early

Watching for ceiling stains

A small stain today prevents drywall replacement tomorrow.

Tenant Education Reduces Emergencies

Many emergencies are caused by misuse.

At move-in, provide simple rules:

Do not flush wipes

Do not pour grease down drains

Report leaks immediately

Change air filters if required

Do not overload outlets

Clear expectations reduce preventable damage.

Build a Contractor Backup List

Emergencies require speed.

Have ready:

Licensed plumber

HVAC technician

Electrician

Roofer

General contractor

Do not search for help at midnight.

Build relationships in advance.

Reliable contractors reduce chaos.

Emergency Fund Rule

Every property should have an emergency reserve.

Minimum recommendation:

Three to six months of operating expenses.

Without reserves, emergencies become financial stress.

With reserves, emergencies become manageable events.

The Prevention Mindset

Emergencies are not random.

They are ignored maintenance.

The landlord who responds early sleeps better.

The landlord who delays pays more.

Prevention costs less than repair.

Every time.

Emergencies will happen occasionally.

But with discipline, they become rare instead of routine.

That is how professionals operate.

Chapter Nine

The 12-Month Maintenance Calendar System

C hecklists are powerful.

But checklists without scheduling become forgotten lists.

This chapter turns everything you've read into a working calendar.

Maintenance only works when it is scheduled.

If it is not on the calendar, it will not get done.

Why a Maintenance Calendar Matters

Landlords get busy.

Rent comes in. Life happens. Repairs stack up.

Without a calendar:

Tasks get delayed

Small issues grow

Seasonal maintenance gets missed

Emergencies increase

A maintenance calendar creates discipline.

Discipline protects profit.

How to Structure Your Year

Divide your year into:

Monthly tasks

Quarterly tasks

Biannual tasks

Annual inspection

Now assign them to real months.

Do not leave them floating.

Sample 12-Month Maintenance Schedule

Use this as a starting point.

Adjust for your climate and property type.

January

Monthly inspection

Check heating system performance

Inspect for ice dam issues

Check interior humidity levels

February

Monthly inspection

Inspect plumbing for freeze damage

Test smoke and carbon monoxide detectors

March

Monthly inspection

Quarterly inspection

Schedule spring HVAC service

Inspect roof after winter weather

April

Monthly inspection

Clean gutters

Inspect exterior grading

Check foundation after snow melt

May

Monthly inspection

Inspect irrigation systems

Pest prevention treatment

June

Monthly inspection

Check air conditioning performance

Inspect exterior paint and siding

July

Monthly inspection

Quarterly inspection

Check water heater performance

Inspect deck and exterior stairs

August

Monthly inspection

Inspect appliances

Check drainage after summer storms

September

Monthly inspection

Schedule fall HVAC service

Inspect roof before winter

Clean gutters

October

Monthly inspection

Biannual water heater flush

Seal exterior cracks

November

Monthly inspection

Quarterly inspection

Check insulation and attic ventilation

Inspect weather stripping

December

Monthly inspection

Review annual maintenance log

Plan next year's capital expenses

Block Scheduling Method

Pick one fixed day per month.

For example:

First Saturday of every month

Third Tuesday of every month

Consistency builds habit.

Habit prevents neglect.

Multi-Property Scheduling

If you own multiple units:

Assign specific weeks per property

Rotate inspections systematically

Use digital reminders

Track completion dates

Do not try to "fit it in."

Schedule it like a meeting.

Digital vs Paper Tracking

You can use:

A printed calendar

Spreadsheet tracker

Property management software

Reminder apps

The tool does not matter.

The habit does.

The Calendar Rule

Never skip two months in a row.

If one month gets missed, double down next month.

Maintenance is cumulative.

Missed inspections stack risk.

Annual Review

At the end of the year:

Review all completed maintenance

Review repair costs

Identify repeat issues

Adjust next year's calendar

Update capital expense forecast

Each year should improve efficiency.

If your system is not improving, it is drifting.

A maintenance calendar turns chaos into structure.

Structure builds predictability.

Predictability builds profit.

Chapter Ten

Budgeting and Repair Reserve Planning

M aintenance is predictable.

Emergencies feel random.

But financially, neither should surprise you.

If you own rental property without a repair reserve, you are gambling.

Professionals do not gamble.

They plan.

The Truth About Repair Costs

Every system in your property has a lifespan.

It will fail eventually.

The only question is whether you are prepared.

Major systems to plan for:

Roof

HVAC

Water heater

Appliances

Flooring

Exterior paint

Plumbing components

None of these last forever.

Ignoring that reality creates financial stress.

The Repair Reserve Rule

Every rental should have a separate repair reserve.

Minimum recommendation:

Five to ten percent of gross monthly rent set aside.

Example:

If rent is $1,500 per month:

Set aside $75–$150 per month.

Do not touch this for anything except property repairs.

This is not optional savings.

It is operational protection.

Emergency Fund vs Repair Reserve

They are not the same.

Repair reserve covers:

Expected replacements

Planned maintenance

Wear and tear

Emergency fund covers:

Insurance deductibles

Major unexpected damage

Vacancy during repairs

Strong landlords keep both.

Capital Expense Forecasting

Look at system ages.

If HVAC is 10 years old, start preparing.

If roof is 18 years old, forecast replacement.

List each major system:

Age

Estimated lifespan

Estimated replacement cost

Years remaining

Divide replacement cost by years remaining.

That number tells you how much to save annually.

Planning removes panic.

Turnover Budgeting

Tenant turnover is guaranteed.

Plan for it.

Budget for:

Paint

Carpet cleaning or replacement

Minor repairs

Cleaning services

Advertising

Assume one month of vacancy every few years.

If you do not plan for turnover, it will hurt.

The Cost of Deferred Maintenance

Landlords who delay repairs pay twice.

Once in damage.

Once in reputation.

Deferred maintenance causes:

Shorter tenant stays

Lower property value

Higher long-term costs

Negative reviews

Cheap today becomes expensive tomorrow.

Tracking Maintenance Expenses

Track every dollar.

Categories to track:

Plumbing

Electrical

HVAC

Appliances

Exterior

General labor

At the end of the year:

Review totals.

Look for patterns.

Recurring problems reveal system weaknesses.

When to Repair vs Replace

Not everything should be patched.

Ask:

Is this repair recurring?

Is the system near end of life?

Will replacement reduce future calls?

Does replacement improve tenant satisfaction?

Sometimes replacement is cheaper long term.

Think beyond today's invoice.

The Discipline Factor

Successful landlords are not lucky.

They are disciplined.

They:

Budget monthly

Save consistently

Forecast replacements

Avoid emotional spending

Review finances annually

Money stress ruins real estate investing.

Planning prevents stress.

The Profit Protection Formula

Rent collected

Minus operating expenses

Minus maintenance

Minus reserves

Equals true profit.

If you are not accounting for maintenance and reserves, your profit number is fake.

Real profit is what remains after preparation.

Rental property is a business.

Businesses require reserves.

Businesses require planning.

If you treat it like a hobby, it will pay like one.

If you treat it like an operation, it will reward you.

Chapter Eleven

Record Keeping and Documentation Systems

If it is not documented, it did not happen.

That is how courts see it.

That is how insurance companies see it.

That is how disputes are decided.

Good documentation protects:

Security deposits

Insurance claims

Legal disputes

Property value

Your reputation

Landlords who document win arguments without arguing.

Why Documentation Matters

Memory is unreliable.

Photos are not.

Receipts are not.

Signed forms are not.

Documentation turns opinion into evidence.

And evidence wins.

What You Should Document

Every property should have records for:

Monthly inspections

Quarterly inspections

Biannual servicing

Annual inspections

Move-in condition reports

Move-out damage reports

Repair invoices

Contractor communication

Tenant maintenance requests

Keep everything.

Storage is cheap.

Lawsuits are not.

Photo Documentation System

Photos are your strongest protection.

Best practice:

Take wide-angle shots first

Take close-up shots second

Include date stamps if possible

Store photos in labeled folders

Organize by:

Property address

Year

Inspection type

Consistency makes retrieval easy later.

Maintenance Logs

Every property should have a maintenance log.

Include:

Date of inspection

Issues found

Repairs completed

Contractor used

Cost

Next service date

A simple spreadsheet works.

A notebook works.

Software works.

The tool is not the priority.

The habit is.

Saving Receipts and Invoices

Save:

HVAC service invoices

Plumbing repairs

Appliance purchases

Roof inspections

Pest control treatments

Keep digital copies.

Back them up.

Insurance companies often request proof of maintenance.

If you have it, claims move faster.

Communication Records

Keep written communication with tenants.

Save:

Maintenance requests

Repair confirmations

Move-in forms

Move-out notices

Security deposit breakdowns

Verbal agreements create problems.

Written records prevent them.

Legal Timeline Awareness

Each state has laws regarding:

Security deposit return deadlines

Repair response requirements

Habitability standards

Know your state's timeline.

Missing deadlines can cost you the entire deposit.

Documentation protects compliance.

Insurance Protection

When filing an insurance claim, you may be asked:

When was the last service?

Was maintenance performed regularly?

Do you have inspection records?

Strong documentation speeds claims.

Weak documentation delays them.

Digital Organization System

Create a folder system:

Property Address

    Inspections

    Repairs

    Invoices

    Photos

Tenant Files

Back it up to cloud storage.

Redundancy prevents loss.

The Professional Standard

Professional landlords operate like property managers.

They:

Log everything

Photograph everything

Save everything

Organize everything

Emotion loses cases.

Documentation wins them.

Rental property is not just about collecting rent.

It is about protecting assets.

Documentation is asset protection.

Every time.

Chapter Twelve

Scaling Maintenance for Multiple Units

One property is manageable.

Two properties require organization.

Five properties require systems.

Ten properties require discipline.

Maintenance that feels simple with one unit becomes chaos without structure as you grow.

Scaling is not about working harder.

It is about building repeatable systems.

The Mindset Shift

When you own multiple units, you are no longer just a landlord.

You are operating a small property management business.

That means:

Standardized checklists

Standardized inspection days

Standardized documentation

Standardized repair procedures

Consistency reduces mistakes.

Mistakes cost money.

Batch Your Maintenance

Do not handle properties randomly.

Batch similar tasks together.

Example:

Week 1: Property A

Week 2: Property B

Week 3: Property C

Week 4: Overflow and repairs

Or:

First Saturday: All monthly inspections

Second Saturday: Repairs and follow-ups

Structure prevents backlog.

Backlog creates emergencies.

Standardize Equipment

Use the same:

HVAC filter sizes when possible

Paint colors

Flooring types

Light fixtures

Appliance brands

Standardization reduces:

Inventory confusion

Replacement delays

Vendor mistakes

Uniform properties are easier to maintain.

Build a Contractor Network

As you scale, relationships matter.

Build a reliable list:

One plumber

One HVAC technician

One electrician

One general contractor

One handyman

Pay on time.

Communicate clearly.

Reliable contractors prioritize reliable landlords.

Track Maintenance Per Property

When scaling, track each unit separately.

Do not lump expenses together.

Track:

Repair frequency

System failures

Tenant damage trends

Operating cost per unit

If one property constantly costs more, investigate why.

Patterns reveal weak assets.

Know When to Delegate

If your time is better spent:

Acquiring properties

Managing finances

Growing portfolio

Consider outsourcing:

Routine maintenance

Lawn care

Snow removal

Inspections

Your time has value.

Calculate it honestly.

Prevent Burnout

Scaling without systems leads to burnout.

Warning signs:

Ignored inspections

Delayed repairs

Frustration with tenants

Cash flow stress

Burnout leads to poor decisions.

Systems protect energy.

Technology Helps, But Discipline Wins

You can use:

Property management software

Maintenance tracking apps

Calendar reminders

Shared contractor platforms

But tools do not replace discipline.

Consistency builds portfolios.

Neglect shrinks them.

Portfolio Review System

Every year, review each property:

Maintenance cost

Repair frequency

Tenant turnover

Capital expense forecast

Net cash flow

If a property consistently underperforms, consider options:

Renovate

Refinance

Raise rent

Sell

Scaling is not about keeping everything forever.

It is about improving performance.

The Scaling Rule

If you cannot manage one property properly, do not buy five.

Build discipline first.

Then build portfolio.

Maintenance systems make scaling possible.

Without them, growth becomes stress.

Scaling is not complicated.

But it requires structure.

Structure protects profit.

Profit funds growth.

Growth builds wealth.

Chapter Thirteen

Conclusion

Maintenance Is Wealth Protection

Rental property is not passive.

It never was.

It is controlled.

And control comes from discipline.

The landlords who struggle are not unlucky.

They are reactive.

They wait.

They postpone.

They hope nothing breaks.

Hope is not a strategy.

Maintenance is.

Every system in your property will fail eventually.

Roofs age.

Water heaters rust.

HVAC systems wear down.

Tenants move out.

None of this is surprising.

The only surprise is whether you prepared for it.

The difference between stressed landlords and profitable landlords is simple:

One reacts.

The other plans.

Monthly inspections prevent small leaks from becoming large repairs.

Quarterly inspections protect structure.

Biannual servicing protects expensive systems.

Annual inspections protect long-term value.

Documentation protects your leverage.

Reserves protect your cash flow.

Systems protect your time.

When you follow the checklists in this book, maintenance stops feeling chaotic.

It becomes predictable.

And predictable is powerful.

Predictable allows you to:

Forecast expenses

Sleep through the night

Handle emergencies calmly

Scale confidently

That is how professionals operate.

Real estate builds wealth slowly.

Maintenance protects that wealth daily.

If you treat your rental like a paycheck, it will eventually cost you.

If you treat it like an asset, it will reward you.

The formula is simple:

Inspect consistently.

Fix small problems immediately.

Document everything.

Save for future repairs.

Operate with discipline.

Do that, and your properties will serve you instead of stress you.

Maintenance is not just about repairs.

It is about protecting income.

It is about protecting time.

It is about protecting freedom.

And that is why it matters.